What others say…

"Greg's poems have been an inspiration to me. I've had many changes in my life and his poems have given me purpose and direction. Greg has uplifted many while skillfully communicating some of life's bittersweet verities. He speaks from the heart and has a God given talent which he shares with many. Love you Mr. Wooley! Keep up the good work!" ~ ***Louise Hawthorne***

"When reading the words that Greg Wooley has written there is something magical that happens. Peace and reassurance are two words that come to mind. Peace that everything is temporary and reassurance that in and through God we are equipped. Greg's work has had a major impact on me professionally and personally! Thanks Greg" ~ ***Anna Reed***

"There have been many times that I have read a poem from Gregory and it just seems to be so heart felt yet I feel as if I could relate in so many ways. They help remind me that life can be full of ups and downs and that if I stay the course it will come out positive in the end. Thank You Greg Wooley for your words of hope & love." ~ ***Donnie Seward***

"God bestowed his grace on Greg. This Grace came with a gift of writing. And Greg shares his gift with us through poetry. Through his own journey, Greg has been able to pen his God given insights into writings, writings that can help each of us on our own paths in this life." ~ ***Sylvia Carrier***

"Greg's intuitions became my into-wishing. This is a sign of rare soul-impacting poetry."
~ ***Elizabeth Perrotta***

"Every sentence of Greg's poems is a haiku, a complete poem independently meaningful."
~ ***Enzo Torre***

"Greg Wooley offers elegant, inspired prose filled with life's wisdom that may be enjoyed and understood by all who read it. Be swept along for the journey." ~ ***Leslie Bertrand***

"Greg's written words are filled with hope. It's the kind of hope that uplifts and touches the core of our being. His poems have moved me deeply because I resonate with them. Greg pours his heart into his words and it shows. Step into his world and let his words embrace you with spirit and uplift you." ~ ***Mark Gai, Podcast Host and Storyteller***

TWINKLING TRINKETS

(RISE AND SHINE SERIES – BOOK 2)

Greg Wooley

Greater Ways Publishing

Twinkling Trinkets by Greg Wooley
Rise and Shine Series – Book 2

Printed in the USA.

ISBN: 978-1-7339478-2-4 (paperback)
ISBN: 978-1-7339478-1-7 (Kindle)

Greater Ways Publishing
PO Box 701017
St. Cloud, FL 34770
GregWooleyBooks@gmail.com
www.GregWooley.com

Disclaimer:

This collection of poems is meant to be inspirational in nature. The author of this book claims no religious training or affiliation with any particular form of religion. While the author hopes these poems might move the reader closer to a relationship with their Creator, he claims no special insight or power.

Permissions:

www.elenadudina.com (cover)
usabookcoach@gmail.com (cover and content coach)
www.facebook.com/DragonsChyldS (wizard)
ID: 592448684 quadshock/shutterstock.com
ID: 89356540 LilKar/shutterstock.com
ID: 85084930 cosma/shutterstock.com

Dedication

This book is dedicated to
Dennis C.

They say that every now and then we get the chance to stand on the shoulders of giants. This can't help but change the way we see things forever. Dennis, I heard about you a month or so before we met. Rumor was, at the outpatient treatment center, you were the one I should ask to be my sponsor. I can remember how scared I was like it was yesterday. I am glad you said yes! No single person has changed my life more, and I am truly grateful. I can't even say you helped me live again, because I never knew life. It's funny that I was always terrified that you were going to tell me what to do, but you never did. You lived it, and gave me an example of someone who I really wanted to be.

I remember the day I was the maddest I ever was when you said, "Every situation you have in your life, good or bad, is because of something you did or something you refused to do!" I had a lot of situations, a lot of situations. In spite of my not thinking that I stood a snowball's chance in hell, I stayed sober because I did what you did. I still do today. If we stand on the shoulder of a giant, our views will be forever changed. My view is forever changed, you were that giant for me. Thank you for being there when I needed you!

Acknowledgments

I am so thankful to God for all the gifts in my life; this book would have never have happened without Him. I am specifically thankful for my wife Monica Wooley. Monica, you have been the greatest at supporting, encouraging and helping me to believe that I am and could be a writer. You always kept believing in me when I didn't believe in myself. I am so thankful I have the gift of these poems bouncing around in my head and for the poem that caught your eye Monica my love. I am grateful for the poem that started our adventure of a life together. I am so very thankful that ...*I wished on that star and had a word with the moon, that God would look down and have you come my way soon.* Who would have ever thought that a poem and a chat on America Online would have us together all these years later? My sweet Argentinian princess, I love you! Thank you for reading all of my poems over the years and for putting up with my daily "read this."

Kerissa, Kirsten, Sunjay and Duranne; my proof-reading team! You guys are absolutely awesome thank you so much for cleaning up my mess. Thank you for your visits when I was in the hospital. Sunjay you have great guitar skills and we rocked the hospital. If you didn't know, that first trip to the hospital was when I became committed to writing every day whether I felt like it or not. I thank you for all of your insights and your proof-reading skills. Ladies thanks you for all the Christmas song parodies and silly rhymes we shared when you were little. I love you!

Luciano Svetlitze thank you for your encouragement and your inspiration. I am so proud of the man you've become. You are proof that hard work, dedication and discipline can make dreams come true. Watching you grow and transform has been a pleasure. You are an amazing son, brother and friend. I'm so glad you came into my life.

Alexander and Ezekiel Wooley thanks for your patience while I've been trying to finish this book.

Arron Rucker, Jason Line and Cindy Noel; my protection from the storm! You guys have made and continually make my life better. Without you guys in my life and your help to alleviate the crazies, I don't think this book would have ever happened.

Travis and Lizette Labell, and our Life Leadership family thank you for the support and inspiration.

Joe LaRosa at LaRosa Coaching thanks for the push to pursue my passions.

Contents

Introduction

Hello my broken friend, I've been waiting for you. Here's a not so secret, secret: I am broken too. In and through that brokenness, I was given the gift of desperation.

In and through that desperation, I was able to admit defeat. Admitting defeat, I was humbled enough to ask for help. By asking for help I was able to start seeking a Power greater than myself. Seeking that Power greater than myself, I was able to start a relationship with a God that I never knew.

"Seek and ye shall find!" And find I did. I hope you have come or are coming to a place where you are seeking too.

In that seeking I have found a meaning and purpose to life that I had never had before. These poems are little pieces of my prayers and thoughts while trying to have a deeper relationship with that Power.

These poems are my little bits of healing and hope for wholeness for myself. These poems are my little bits of hope for healing for others. I truly believe we all have hidden gems of wisdom in our hearts. I pray these gems of mine help you to dig in to your depths and discover the gems within yourself. Thanks for letting me share these Twinkling Trinkets from my heart.

I am Who I am

I am who I am and I'm not who I'm not
I once knew who I was but I somehow forgot

There is so much to learn, yet much more to forget
I'll not be identified by remorse and regret

I am not what I've done and I'm not what I do
There are many layers to peel to find the real you

I am not this body, I am not this mortal shell
I am not identified by the times that I've been
through sheer hell

I am not these scars and I am not the old bruises
A person is so often identified by the choices he
chooses

Sometimes we need to take time to unravel the mess
So when we're asked who we are it's not just a guess

Let me dig past the pride and sort through my fears
To the me that has been there for all of these years

When I surrender it all in the dead of the night
I know there is a real God and I am His light

I remembered that I am His hope and I am true love
We are meant to share healing from our God above

Perhaps it's come time that you remember that you
forgot too
You're not what you've done and you are not what
you do

Twinkling Trinkets

Like little twinkling trinkets washed up on the beach
We never really know just who we're meant to reach

We spent days lost and lonely, it's coming time to shine
Messes can be made messages when we give in to the Divine.

God's light reflects upon you, and everyone but you can see
It's only the voices inside your head that keep you from all you were meant to be

Now you reflect the Sonlight and you're washed upon the shore
Your rough edges have been softened and God's calling you for more

Now that you're on dry land and you've been delivered from the wave
Don't let your habits and your old thinking keep calling you a slave

We are like little twinkling trinkets washed up on the beach
If we are willing to put out our hands, God will choose who we reach

Came and Went

Friends have come and friends have went
Friends like you they are heaven sent!

A gift from God that keeps on giving
You, my friend, make life worth living

We share some laughs, we share some tears
And with friends like you I can share my fears

When I am no good you call me good enough
You keep me walking when the road gets tough

You help give me faith that my hurts will mend
I am ever grateful that I can call you friend

Prayer and Meditation

Prayer and meditation, meditation and prayer
God, I offer my thoughts and my will into Your care

It seems my own best thinking always leads me astray
I offer you my heart and my mind as I start out the day

Lead me to the path that is the way I should walk
I pray I might be Your voice with every word that I talk

Prayer and meditation, meditation and prayer
God you give the blessings that we're meant to share

Out of the Box

I'm out of the box and I'm breaking the dam
I'm discovering new depths in the person I am

Self-deception deceives and I don't think that I'm alone
How many times are we blocked by what we think we have known

In easing God out, I turn myself in to Him
In the shadow of my self-serving Ego, my light starts to go dim

The box and the dam they become like a black hole
The ways of this world they suck the life from my soul

I think what I think about and feel what I feel
How much is perception, how much is for real

In the box it's about me and the dam it's blocking my view
I know what I know and there is no room for the new

I had to get out of the box and break down my God dam
To unlock the real me and discover the shining soul that I am

Into the Flow

Out of the mud and into the flow
I greet the sun rise as a new chance to grow

The breath that we breathe, the water we drink
What we hear and we see; shape the thoughts that
we think

Our little daily habits are ever plotting our course
Are we moving away from, or embracing the
Source?

A spiritual malady needs a spiritual solution
We all need a break from the mass souls pollution

The world it bombards with its constant bad news
What we see and we hear is our choice to choose

Now I'm not really saying to stick your head in the
sand
It's our everyday choices that lead to all God's
planned

Let's get out of the mud and climb out of the mire
And be the best we can be and lead lives that inspire

Can You See

Most of us have vision yet so few of us can see
See a picture of the future and all that we can be

I pray you awaken today and dare to remember your dream
A life without a dream should cause a nightmarish scream

A scream out to the Creator "God my God, why am I here?!"
Give me vision and purpose, Lord help me to see clear

Father you've given me eyes yet still I've been blind
Let me see with my heart and create with my mind

The Hole

We have a restlessness that just can't seem to be stilled
Stemming from a God-sized hole that needs to be filled

We fill it with addictions and we fill it with greed
Quieting the restlessness alone, we cannot succeed

Until we can surrender, open our hearts, and give God our will
Only then will our restlessness subside, will our souls then be still

And then in the stillness we'll hear the whispers of His voice
How we fill the void within us has ever been our choice

Sea of Serenity

Floating in a river of peace flowing towards serenity's sea
Lord transform these defects of character that are infecting me

I float for some moments but then I can't help but stop and remember
When it comes to God's kingdom I've not always been the best member

So many of my talents have gone unused and they've rusted
And I've done but a fraction with the gifts that He's entrusted

Today is the day and the past is passed I will begin again
My peace won't be bothered by my remembering when

Swimming in the sea of serenity I'll dare to make a wave
Sharing a wave that when defects become assets they no longer can enslave

By Loving You

I am loving God when I am loving you
Let's be pipeline that Love's flowing through

Clear the channel and be at peace
The past and future we'll just release

Here and now, we will just be
I am with Him and He with me

If I love my brothers and sisters that I can see
It shows my love for God and His love for me

I am loving God by loving all
Today I'll answer Love, when Love comes to call

Converse Among the Wise

How I long to walk and converse with the wise
To help me cast a vision and to open my eyes

Open my eyes to the strengths and the me I cannot see
To make a difference in this world and be all I can be

Lord lead me to relationships that will make me my absolute best
As the seeds of hope in me grow, lead me to others who would be blessed

A blessing is not a blessing until that blessing is given away
How I long to converse with the wise and walk in their way

Retreat

Sometimes I need to take a momentary retreat
More than a surrender or admission of defeat

A time alone with God, a needed getaway
So I can hear His whispers and take some time to pray

The world it likes to keep us busy, busy, busy as a bee
In the chaos and the noise I lose the heart of me

Sometimes we need to take an intentional time for a time out
To find our way back to center, God renews us inside out

Hands Bound

Our lost time it can be never found
That clock's hands, they have us bound

Some of the things we're willing to trade for our time
When our days are done they will seem like a crime

A great crime to God, to family, and to our fellow man
What could we have accomplished if we'd had a plan?

A failure to plan is a sure plan to fail
Don't be left standing on the dock when your dreams they set sail

Our time lost can it never be it found
Take time to dream and to live before your clock has unwound

Out of the Pit

Out of the pit and on to the ladder
I started taking the steps to a life that might really matter

I'm cutting the anchor, I'm dropping the stone
I need to take time, a time for my God alone

To talk without resentment or the pain of the past
Help me to let go and to find freedom at last

Out of the pit and on to new ground
God help me to keep stepping forward in this new life I have found

Cracks

There are cracks in my walls, there are cracks in my shell
Imprisoned in this comfort zone, it's my self-imposed hell

There were cracks in my foundation that I had to patch
No one gets through life without a bruise or a scratch

Sometimes I get so down and think this life isn't what it's cracked up to be
Then I had to come to the realization these cracks were making me

Each one us have our faults and often hidden brokenness down in our core
Our egos want them hidden, yet in the open they can make us so much more

I pray your shell might crack to let your inner light shine bright
It's through surrendering to our brokenness we can win the fight

The Battle Between My Ears

There's an ever waging war; a battle between my ears
Wrestling with my selfishness, my resentments, and my fears

The problem always is, for me, myself and I
I start looking at myself and forget about my why

You see we are all created with gifts that our Creator gave
And there is a hurting someone out there that your story's meant to save

You've overcome so much yet still you wallow and you whine
The grapes that are fertilized are the sweetest of the vine

You are a new creation; now take it as a fact
You are a walking testimony; be more Christ like when you act

Open Your Eyes

Come now dreamer open your eyes
Not everyone lives, yet everyone dies

Don't take for granted not one single breath
Live life to the fullest until it's time to face death

There is laughter to share and there are tears to be shed
Your dreams can come to life if only they would get fed

God gave us our dreams, so many leave them to sleep
When the angels look down, I'm sure that they weep

Come now dreamer it's time that you live
The world needs the gift that you're meant to give

Shine Your Light

Shine your light like a Hope shining beacon high up on a hill
So the world can see the difference when we live in God's will

God didn't give us light so we would hide it ‘neath a shade
In His renewing and restoring, there's a difference to be made

A difference to be made that you are meant to make
So shine your light brightly like there are lives at stake

Lord I thank you for the light that You've lit in me
I pray to do Your will and work in setting people free

Attention Paid

Are you paying attention to the attention you pay
There are so many distractions that are distracting
today

Our primary purpose it is losing its prime
By all the distractions that are wasting our time

We flip through the channels or scroll and scroll
through the post
Never thinking about what we see and hear is what
hurts us the most

It's voluntary dream slaughter we are committing
ourselves
As we leave our dreams dying in our minds' back
shelves

I will take time to read and I will take time to right
So I will be armed and equipped to give my dreams
flight

Today I will pay attention to the attention I've paid
It's through our daily habits that our future's
foundation is laid

Bridges Burned

Some bridges get built and other bridges get burned
We need to make sure to reflect when we've lived and we've learned

When my history is forgotten, it's sure to repeat
For the rest of my life I prefer my bridges complete

We build a new bridge with every conversation and shake of a hand
Never knowing where that bridge might take us, or what the future has planned

To get to where we are going there's sure to be bridges we need
We need to be a builder of relationships if we are to succeed

I am Recovery

I don't care about your religion, I don't care about your race
I don't care about your politics or what you think of as your place

It really doesn't matter your job, your race, your creed
I whisper with sweet lies, just one is what you need

Perhaps you think you're different: maybe better, maybe worse
Deceiving and self-deception have ever been my curse

You're easily distracted, forgetting the truth that set you free
I will be your master, with just one and YOU BELONG TO ME

Addiction is ever patient, just waiting for the day
For when our purpose prime is lost, we get lost along the way

I am addictions enemy, I am here to set you free
I don't care about your creed or color, I am Recovery

From powerless to power-filled rebuilding on the way
I will give reprieve but only for today

I am an end to loneliness, to misery and despair
I am named RECOVERY, come step into my care

Special Excerpt

Inspiration from Greg Wooley's book:

GEMS from G.O.D.

The Shiniest of Diamonds

The shiniest of diamonds come from the blackest of
coal
The wisest of wisdom comes from the most
damaged soul

So many times things are not just as they look
We can't judge the soup before it's had time to cook

Embracing your pains, your misery and your
brokenness
The transformation of your story is your chance to
bless

Going through hell doesn't mean that you're there to
stay
May every hurt be turned into compassion for
another on this very day

It takes time and severe pressure for a diamond to
transform
I pray you washed and made new at the end of the
storm

Something so hard yet so precious is transformed
from the blackest of coal
There are diamonds waiting to be uncovered from
every hurt in the depth of your soul

Our Most Valuable Asset

Some cherish their diamonds, others value their pearls
A country's most valuable asset is its young boys and girls
For what use is a full coin purse or a vault full of gold
If we're left without love when we're dying and old
Teach the children well and set them well on the way
To insure a brighter tomorrow and a much better today
When it comes down to it our greatest natural resource
Are our young men and women set well on their course
So take the time to teach and take the time to care
We are all on a journey a journey that we are meant to share
So for the sake of today and for the hopes of tomorrow
Help teach our young well and keep them from sorrow
More precious than diamonds, so much warmer than gold
Is a love that gives back when we've grown weary and old

Love Is

Love is our foundation, our walls and Love is our ceiling
Love is who we are, Love is so much more than a feeling

Love can make us cry and Love can call us to action
Love makes us shine a little brighter with the law of attraction

When you look into the mirror, I pray you'd see a picture of Love
A living, loving, active image of our God above

Love is our foundation, our walls and Love is our floor
Love transforms the willing if we'll step through Love's door

The Cross Road

We stand at the cross road of hope and despair
When it comes to trouble we've all had our share

Narrow is the gate and straight is the way
I pray that you rise above the chaos on this very day

May you have one foot in heaven and one on the earth
And dare to dig through your layers and discover your worth

We are not what we've done and not what we did
Many go through a lifetime with their identity hid

Everything in this perishing world will come to a loss
I pray the you discover your being at the heart of the cross

May you be stripped clean to your own naked truth
And dream once again as in the days of your youth

Dream the dreams of who they told you should be
Dare to dream dreams of the joyous and free

So then at hope and despair you come to the center
The kingdom of God is waiting for you to come enter

God’s Gold

Value, oh value do you know what you’re worth
God had you in mind from before your own birth

So much to learn, so much more to forget
Let's let the past be the past and let go of regret

Today is the day a great gift of the present
I won't be caught in replay with what I resent

I'll take charge of my mind and of my minds state
I'll act in positive action not relying on fate

I will take some moments to think and be still
And offer my life up to do my God's will

Do you know your own value, you are worth more than gold

I pray you bring a smile to God's face when your story is told

Value, oh value do you know what you’re worth
God had you in mind before the day of your birth

Cause of Death

The number one cause of death has always been
birth
Do you let the temporary things of world give you
your worth

As we go about in pursuit of our why and the doing
our how
May you have the gift of the present and value the
now

If we really want to live then we must give our life
away
The real path to eternity is making the most of today

The number one cause of death has always been
birth
Our life is a gift of the Creator nothing can add or
take away from our worth

Real Eyes

Realize, real eyes help me to see
How I'm bound by selfishness and can't seem to break free

I'm in my own way it seems I am my own storm
God free me from the bondage of self in its every form

My ego is inflated and I'm all puffed up with selfish pride
Then the voices of inferiority whisper your ego has lied

The ride on the self-centered cycle it baffles my brains
I end back where I started bound by selfishness's chains

Realize, real eyes help me to see
How I might think more of others and a little less of me

Life Rope

God speaks to those who are longing to hear
Let me step into faith and step past my fear

Lord give me a vision that leads to a new road
The present has me weary, I need help with my load

I long for Your Highways paved with purpose and hope
As You pull me ahead let me be Your life rope

A life rope to the hopeless and those that despair
I give my past, present and future into Your care
Every good blessing You give is a blessing to share

In Fear I Am

Inferior, in fear I am
Fear it acts like a big God dam

I can't move forward and I can't move back
How many times will fear get me off my track

I know it's illusion and it's not really real
Just how many dreams does fear come to steal

It calls you less when you should be called more
It says don't knock when you stand at the door

The door of opportunity it stays closed tight
Every time we dare let fear win in faith's fight

I pray you'd dare to make courage your new friend
And the damn dam of fear would finally end

The river of the spirit then would start to flow
Then the adventures we'd have and places we could go!

Inferior, in fear I am not
In faithfulness my fear is forgot

Paths

Each and every day there are but two paths to take
We can choose selfishness or live for God's sake

Am I serving myself or in service to my Higher Power
My ways bring loneliness, His bring joy unto my last hour

There's something about us giving that it sets our souls free
I pray I choose the path that lets me be all He'd have me be

Author Biography

Greg Wooley has been in the self-help field for over twenty-five years. That's when the journey to overcome a seemingly hopeless and helpless state of mind started.

He has found victory over addiction and depression. One of the best ways to stay on the hope filled path is by helping others to find their way to hope as well. Helping others find hope is where Greg has found his purpose and passion.

He truly hopes these poetic gems will help take your eyes off the problems and shine some light on the solutions. He has written personal poems for keepsakes, vows and presents.

He has also partnered with pastors to use his poems in their sermons and growth messages. Greg would love to hear from you and is very interested in finding ways to share in shining the light of hope together. His life is a great testimony of hope, healing and overcoming the odds.

Greg love's building and growing communities for both personal and professional growth. Like-minded people with like-minded goals is where real life change happens!

Contact Greg at www.GregWooley.com.

Ordering Information

Greater Ways Publishing
PO Box 701017
St. Cloud, FL 34770
GregWooleyBooks@gmail.com
www.GregWooley.com

Twinkling Trinkets
ISBN: 978-1-7339478-1-7
(Kindle)
ISBN: 978-1-7339478-2-4
(Paperback)

Gems from G.O.D.
ISBN: 978-1-7339478-9-3
(paperback)
ISBN: 978-1-7339478-7-9
(case laminate)
ISBN: 978-1-7339478-8-6
(Kindle)

www.ingramcontent.com/pod-product-compliance
Lightning Source LLC
LaVergne TN
LVHW050946080826
845145LV00004B/1434

* 9 7 8 1 7 3 3 9 4 7 8 2 4 *